Lerner SPORTS

SUPER SPORTS
TEAMS

INSIDE THE PHILADELPHIA EAGLES

JOSH ANDERSON

Lerner Publications ◆ Minneapolis

SPORTS THRILLS
MEET
RESEARCH SKILLS

Lerner SPORTS

Free Database Trial: **lernersports.com**

Lerner Publications Company
An imprint of Lerner Publishing Group, Inc.
241 First Avenue North
Minneapolis, MN 55401 USA

For reading levels and more information, look up this title at www.lernerbooks.com.

Main body text set in Aptifer Slab LT Pro / Typeface provided by Linotype AG

Library of Congress Cataloging-in-Publication Data

Names: Anderson, Josh, author.
Title: Inside the Philadelphia Eagles / Josh Anderson.
Description: Minneapolis : Lerner Publications, [2024] | Series: Lerner sports. Super sports teams | Includes bibliographical references and index. | Audience: Ages 7–11 | Audience: Grades 4–6 | Summary: "The Philadelphia Eagles are known for their dark-green uniforms and passionate fan base. Find out why fans are so loyal to the Eagles by exploring the team's history, greatest moments, and superstar players"—Provided by publisher.
Identifiers: LCCN 2022052064 (print) | LCCN 2022052065 (ebook) | ISBN 9781728491035 (library binding) | ISBN 9798765604069 (paperback) | ISBN 9798765601679 (ebook)
Subjects: LCSH: Philadelphia Eagles (Football team)—History—Juvenile literature.
Classification: LCC GV956.P44 A55 2024 (print) | LCC GV956.P44 (ebook) | DDC 796.332/640974811—dc23/eng/20221104

LC record available at https://lccn.loc.gov/2022052064
LC ebook record available at https://lccn.loc.gov/2022052065

Manufactured in the United States of America
2-1010515-51052-1/8/2024

TABLE OF
CONTENTS

Eagles fans cheer for their team in the 2018 Super Bowl.

SUPER BOWL CHAMPS

FACTS AT A GLANCE

- The **EAGLES** started playing in 1933.

- Philadelphia won its first National Football League (NFL) **CHAMPIONSHIP** in 1948 when the team defeated the Chicago Cardinals 7–0.

- The Eagles played in the **SUPER BOWL** for the first time in 1981.

- The Eagles **FIRST WON** the Super Bowl in 2018.

All season long, the Philadelphia Eagles had high hopes of winning the 2018 Super Bowl. For only the second time in team history, the Eagles won 13 games. They finished the regular season as one of the best teams in the NFL. But one of those wins came with a big loss to the team. Quarterback Carson Wentz was injured and could not finish the season.

Many Eagles fans thought the team's Super Bowl dreams were over. But Nick Foles stepped into the role and led the Eagles through the playoffs. Philadelphia's Super Bowl dream became a reality.

Most people thought quarterback Tom Brady and the New England Patriots would be too much for Philadelphia to handle. Brady had led his team to five Super Bowl victories. One of those wins was the year before, when Brady and the Patriots made the biggest Super Bowl comeback of all time. But Foles and the Eagles were ready.

The Eagles led for most of the game. With about nine minutes left in the fourth quarter, Brady threw a touchdown pass that gave the Patriots a 33–32 lead. Over the next seven minutes, Foles and the Eagles drove down the field toward the end zone.

On a third-down play from the 11-yard line, Foles noticed tight end Zach Ertz covered by only one Patriots defender. Ertz crossed toward the middle of the field, and Foles fired a pass to him. Ertz made the catch. The Patriots defender dove, hoping to tackle Ertz before he scored. But Ertz leaped into the air and landed in the end zone. The Eagles took a 38–33 lead with less than three minutes to play.

Hoping for another big comeback, Brady and the Patriots drove toward the end zone. But Eagles defensive end Brandon Graham sacked Brady and caused the quarterback to fumble. The Eagles recovered the ball and went on to win 41–33. After starting the season as the team's backup, Foles threw three touchdowns and caught a touchdown pass in the Super Bowl. He won the game's Most Valuable Player (MVP) award. Fans in Philadelphia could finally celebrate their team's first Super Bowl victory.

Zach Ertz (*left*) dives into the end zone to give the Eagles the lead in the 2018 Super Bowl.

Nick Foles went from backup quarterback to Super Bowl MVP in 2018.

Clyde Simmons recorded 76 sacks in eight seasons with the Eagles.

FLY EAGLES, FLY!

In 1933, President Franklin D. Roosevelt started the National Recovery Administration (NRA). The group's goal was to help Americans during the Great Depression (1929–1939). The Great Depression was a time when many people could not find jobs and did not have enough money for things they needed. The NRA's symbol was an eagle.

The National Recovery Administration's eagle symbol inspired Philadelphia's team name.

Bert Bell and Lud Wray owned a pro football team in Philadelphia, Pennsylvania. When they chose the team's name, they were inspired by the NRA's symbol. The Philadelphia Eagles joined the NFL in 1933. Bell served as president. Wray was the team's first head coach.

In the NFL's early days, teams with the most money usually signed the best college players. This made it hard for other teams to get better. In 1935, Bell suggested that the NFL hold a draft where teams would take turns picking new players. The first NFL Draft took place in 1936, and the yearly event continues today.

The Eagles and the Chicago Bears play a game in 1941.

Eagles head coach Earle "Greasy" Neale (*top*) holds a team meeting on an airplane in 1945.

The Eagles struggled in their first years in the NFL. In 1941, the team hired Earle "Greasy" Neale as its head coach. Neale helped the Eagles improve during the 1940s.

Many NFL players left their teams to join the US military during World War II (1939–1945). In 1943, neither the Eagles nor the Pittsburgh Steelers had enough players for a full team. The teams decided to play together for one season. The unofficial name for the combined team was the Steagles. In 1944, the Eagles and Steelers began competing as single teams again.

Steve Van Buren (*left*) tries to avoid defenders during a 1948 game.

From 1947 to 1949, the Eagles played in three straight NFL Championship Games. The team's best player during this time was running back Steve Van Buren. But Philadelphia lost the 1947 championship to the Chicago Cardinals 28–21.

In 1948, the Eagles matched up with the Cardinals again in the championship game. This time, Philadelphia won their first league title 7–0. The next year, the Eagles won again. They defeated the Los Angeles Rams in the 1949 NFL Championship Game 14–0.

Eagles wide receiver Pete Pihos (*right*) makes a catch in a 1948 game against the Los Angeles Rams.

Chuck Bednarik entered the Pro Football Hall of Fame in 1967 after a 14-year career with the Eagles.

AMAZING MOMENTS

After three straight trips to the NFL Championship Game from 1947 to 1949, the Eagles failed to finish in first place again for ten years. Led by two veteran players, the Eagles made it back to the NFL Championship Game in 1960. Quarterback Norm Van Brocklin and offensive lineman and linebacker Chuck Bednarik were two of the most famous stars of the time. Bednarik had starred for the Eagles for more than a decade on both offense and defense.

The Eagles defeated the Green Bay Packers 17–13 in the 1960 NFL Championship Game. The first Super Bowl was in 1967. But the Eagles didn't play in the Super Bowl for many years.

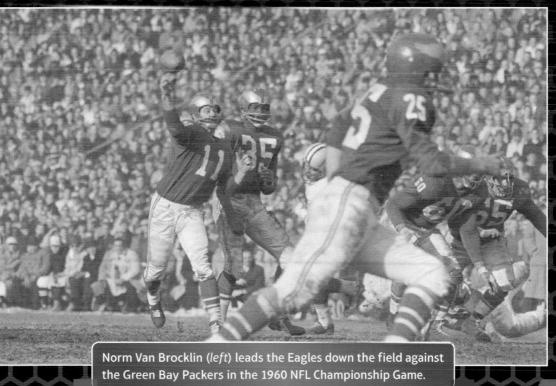

Norm Van Brocklin (*left*) leads the Eagles down the field against the Green Bay Packers in the 1960 NFL Championship Game.

The team hired Dick Vermeil as head coach in 1976. He led the Eagles to two playoff appearances in 1978 and 1979. The next season, the Eagles advanced to the Super Bowl for the first time.

The team's opponent in the 1981 Super Bowl was the Oakland Raiders. Most people expected the Eagles to win. But Philadelphia fell behind 14–0 in the first quarter and couldn't make a comeback. The Raiders won the game 27–10.

Quarterback Ron Jaworski helped lead the Eagles to the 1981 Super Bowl.

After 1981, the Eagles went through another long period without reaching the Super Bowl. Andy Reid became Philadelphia's head coach in 1999. The team improved quickly under Reid. From 2002 to 2005, the Eagles played in four straight National Football Conference (NFC) Championship Games. They lost the first three, barely missing out on the Super Bowl.

In 2005, the Eagles faced the Atlanta Falcons for the NFC Championship. Philadelphia's defense made sure the team didn't lose again. The Eagles sacked Falcons quarterback Michael Vick four times and took the ball from him once, holding the Falcons to only 10 points in the game. The 27–10 victory sent the Eagles to the Super Bowl for the first time since 1981. Although they lost the 2005 Super Bowl to the New England Patriots, fans watched a very exciting game. New England came out on top 24–21.

Reid left the team after the 2012 season. The Eagles have continued to be successful without him. After winning the 2018 Super Bowl, the Eagles made the playoffs in four of the next five seasons.

Philadelphia finished the 2022 season first in the NFC and returned to the Super Bowl. They faced the Kansas City Chiefs and Philadelphia's former coach, Andy Reid. Although the teams were evenly matched throughout the game, the Chiefs kicked a field goal in the final seconds and won 38–35.

Andy Reid (*right*) coached the Eagles for 14 seasons.

Randall Cunningham finished his career with 4,928 rushing yards. That's the third most by a quarterback in NFL history.

EAGLES SUPERSTARS

Many incredible players played for the Eagles over the years. Running back Steve Van Buren was the team's first superstar. Supersonic Steve led the NFL in rushing yards and rushing touchdowns four times. The Hall of Famer was the key player when the Eagles won the 1948 and 1949 NFL Championships.

Steve Van Buren runs with the ball. He led the NFL in rushing four times.

Most NFL stars play either offense or defense. Chuck Bednarik was an all-time great offensive lineman and a skilled linebacker for the Philadelphia defense. The Hall of Famer played for the Eagles for his entire 14-year career. He was a Pro Bowl player eight times.

Reggie White was one of the greatest defensive ends ever to play football. The Minister of Defense played his first eight seasons with the Eagles. White led the NFL in sacks twice during his time in Philadelphia. For his career, his 198 sacks rank second all-time.

Reggie White entered the Pro Football Hall of Fame in 2006.

Donovan McNabb led the Eagles to 92 regular season wins in his 11 years with the team.

Two exciting quarterbacks spent most of their careers with the Eagles. Randall Cunningham's running skills were unique. He was also a good passer, making him nearly impossible to defend. Cunningham led the Eagles to the playoffs five times in his 11 seasons with the team.

With Donovan McNabb at quarterback, the Eagles were often one of the top-scoring teams in the NFL. McNabb leads all Eagles quarterbacks in passing yards and passing touchdowns. He led the Eagles to the playoffs eight times between 1999 and 2009. McNabb was a Pro Bowl player six times during his career.

LeSean McCoy led the NFL with 20 touchdowns in 2011.

Safety Brian Dawkins was McNabb's teammate for many years. Dawkins's 34 interceptions are tied for the most ever by an Eagles player. The Hall of Famer was a Pro Bowl player nine times.

In the modern NFL, it's common for running backs to catch as many passes as wide receivers do. But it was not common when Brian Westbrook joined the Eagles in 2002. Westbrook helped coaches see the value of running backs who were skilled pass catchers. He led the NFL in combined rushing and receiving yards in 2007.

In 2008, running back LeSean McCoy joined the team. He took over for Westbrook, who left the Eagles in 2009. McCoy led the NFL in rushing yards in 2013 and finished his Eagles career as the team's all-time leading rusher.

Brian Westbrook (*left*) avoids a Denver Broncos defender as he runs toward the end zone.

Jalen Hurts threw four touchdown passes in a game for the first time in 2022 against the Pittsburgh Steelers.

LET'S GO, EAGLES!

After finishing in last place in 2020, the Eagles made some big changes. In 2021, the team hired Nick Sirianni to be its new head coach. Sirianni had served as an assistant coach for three other NFL teams before going to Philadelphia.

Sirianni made backup Jalen Hurts the team's starting quarterback. Hurts continues the Philadelphia tradition of quarterbacks who are great runners. The speedy Hurts led all NFL quarterbacks with 784 rushing yards and 10 rushing touchdowns in 2021.

Nick Sirianni talks to players and other coaches through his headset during Eagles games.

The Eagles picked wide receiver DeVonta Smith in the 2021 NFL Draft. Smith won the 2020 Heisman Trophy as the year's best player in college football. With a greatly improved offense in 2021, Philadelphia finished with a 9–8 record and made the playoffs.

Heading into 2022, the Eagles traded for A. J. Brown, one of the NFL's best wide receivers. Brown's size and speed help him make amazing catches. When he has the ball, his strength makes him hard to tackle.

The Eagles have three 2021 Pro Bowlers on defense. Defensive linemen Josh Sweat and Javon Hargrave each had 7.5 sacks in 2021. Four-time Pro Bowl cornerback Darius Slay is one of the best in the NFL at stopping wide receivers. The team also added defensive lineman Jordan Davis from the University of Georgia.

The Eagles were one of the NFL's top teams in 2022. Although they lost the Super Bowl, fans know the team has what it takes to return to the big game in the near future.

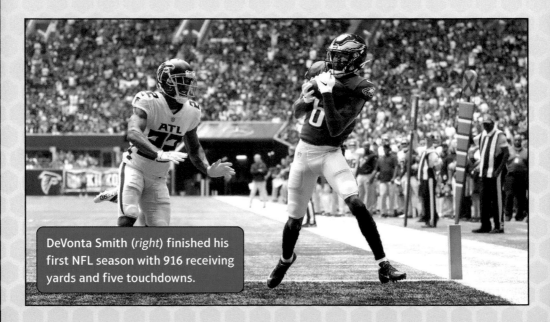

DeVonta Smith (*right*) finished his first NFL season with 916 receiving yards and five touchdowns.

A. J. Brown joined the Eagles in 2022 after three seasons with the Tennessee Titans.

In 2013, LeSean McCoy rushed for 217 yards in a game against the Detroit Lions.

EAGLES
SEASON RECORD HOLDERS

RUSHING TOUCHDOWNS

1. LeSean McCoy, 17 (2011)
2. Steve Van Buren, 15 (1945)
3. Steve Van Buren, 13 (1947)
   Ricky Watters, 13 (1996)
4. Steve Van Buren, 11 (1949)
   Tom Sullivan, 11 (1974)
   Ricky Watters, 11 (1995)
   Miles Sanders, 11 (2022)

RECEIVING TOUCHDOWNS

1. Terrell Owens, 14 (2004)
2. Tommy McDonald, 13 (1960)
   Tommy McDonald, 13 (1961)
   Mike Quick, 13 (1983)
3. Eight players tied with 11 receiving touchdowns

PASSING YARDS

1. Carson Wentz, 4,039 (2019)
2. Donovan McNabb, 3,916 (2008)
3. Donovan McNabb, 3,875 (2004)
4. Randall Cunningham, 3,808 (1988)
5. Carson Wentz, 3,782 (2016)

RUSHING YARDS

1. LeSean McCoy, 1,607 (2013)
2. Wilbert Montgomery, 1,512 (1979)
3. Ricky Watters, 1,411 (1996)
4. Wilbert Montgomery, 1,402 (1981)
5. Brian Westbrook, 1,333 (2007)

PASS COMPLETIONS

1. Carson Wentz, 388 (2019)
2. Carson Wentz, 379 (2016)
3. Sam Bradford, 346 (2015)
4. Donovan McNabb, 345 (2008)
5. Donovan McNabb, 330 (2000)

SACKS

1. Reggie White, 21 (1987)
2. Clyde Simmons, 19 (1992)
3. Reggie White, 18 (1986)
   Reggie White, 18 (1988)
   Jason Babin, 18 (2011)
4. Greg Brown, 16 (1984)
   Haason Reddick, 16 (2022)

GLOSSARY

comeback: when a team that is losing recovers to tie or win the game

cornerback: a defender whose main job is to prevent pass catches

defensive end: a player whose main jobs are to rush the quarterback and defend rushing plays

defensive lineman: a player at the front of the defense

end zone: the area at each end of a football field where players score touchdowns

fumble: when a football player loses hold of the ball while handling or running with it

Hall of Famer: a player honored in the Pro Football Hall of Fame in Canton, Ohio

linebacker: a defender who usually plays in the middle of the defense

offensive lineman: a player at the front of the offense whose job is to block defensive players

Pro Bowl: the NFL's all-star game

sack: to tackle the quarterback for a loss of yards

tight end: a player whose main jobs are to block defenders and catch passes

LEARN MORE

Goodman, Michael. *Philadelphia Eagles*. Mankato, MN: The Creative Company, 2023.

Philadelphia Eagles
https://www.philadelphiaeagles.com

Pro Football Hall of Fame: Philadelphia Eagles
https://www.profootballhof.com/teams/philadelphia–eagles/

Scheff, Matt. *The Super Bowl: Football's Game of the Year*. Minneapolis: Lerner Publications, 2021.

Sports Illustrated Kids—Football
https://www.sikids.com/football

Stabler, David. *Aaron Donald vs. Reggie White: Who Would Win?* Minneapolis: Lerner Publications, 2024.

INDEX

PHOTO ACKNOWLEDGMENTS

Image credits: Mitchell Leff/Stringer/Getty Images, p.4; Gregory Shamus/Staff/Getty Images, p.6; TIMOTHY A. CLARY/Contributor/Getty Images, p.7; Stephen Dunn/Staff/Getty Images, p.8; Bettmann/Contributor/Getty Images, p.9; Bettmann/Contributor/Getty Images, p.10; Bettmann/Contributor/Getty Images, p.11; Nate Fine/Contributor/Getty Images, p.12; Vic Stein/Contributor/Getty Images, p.13; Robert Riger/Contributor/Getty Images, p.14; Bettmann/Contributor/Getty Images, p.15; Focus On Sport/Contributor/Getty Images, p.16; Sporting News Archive/Contributor/Getty Images, p.17; Ronald C. Modra/Contributor/Getty Images, p.18; Bettmann/Contributor/Getty Images, p.19; Focus On Sport/Contributor/Getty Images, p.20; George Gojkovich/Contributor/Getty Images, p.21; Al Bello/Staff/Getty Images, p.22; Hunter Martin/Contributor/Getty Images, p.23; Tim Nwachukwu/Staff/Getty Images, p.24; Tim Nwachukwu/Staff/Getty Images, p.25; Todd Kirkland/Stringer/Getty Images, p.26; Mitchell Leff/Contributor/Getty Images, p.27; Focus On Sport/Contributor/Getty Images, p.28;

Design element: Master3D/Shutterstock.com.

Cover image: Rey Del Rio/Stringer/Getty Images